# Heaven's Comforts
# for the Grieving Soul

By Candyce DuPont Magee

Heaven's Comforts for the Grieving Soul
Copyright © 2013 by Candyce DuPont Magee

Editorial assistance by Kristin Magee

# Prologue

A man is walking down the street when he falls into a hole. The walls are so steep he can't get out. A doctor passes by, and the guy shouts up, "Hey, you! Can you help me out?" The doctor writes a prescription, throws it down into the hole, and moves on.

Then a priest comes along, and the guy shouts up, "Father, I'm down in the hole. Can you help me out?" The priest writes out a prayer, throws it down into the hole, and moves on.

Then a friend walks by: "Hey Joe, it's me. Can you help me out?" And the friend jumps into the hole. Our guy says, "Are you stupid? Now we're both down here."

The friend says, "Yeah, but I've been down here before, and I know the way out."

This is a clever little story[1] but also undeniably true. Once we fall into grief, when we don't know how to get out of the hole of sorrow and despair over the loss of a loved one, we need a friend to show us the path to life again. In this book you and I will journey through the Scriptures together, seeking a

---

1   The West Wing, Episode 32, "Noel"

way out of our present darkness into the light of God's eternal gift of Heaven. Together we will see that the only lasting and satisfying solution to our grief is to fix our eyes upon God as He demonstrates His care for us through His Word.

# Writing an Introduction

I find myself in a very ironic situation. I have to write an introduction to a book on Heaven after struggling for years with doubts about its very existence. Fortunately, I am in good company. C.S. Lewis also found himself fighting disbelief: "You never know how much you really believe anything until its truth or falsehood becomes a matter of life and death to you."[2] This is my experience; this is my challenge.

So how did I come to write this book? I lost someone very dear to me, my twenty-two-year-old son. It wasn't until the initial shock of his death wore off that I could even begin to process what I did and did not believe. Spiritual anesthesia is a wonderful mercy, but it doesn't last forever. Little by little and in various ways, the notion of life after death crept into my consciousness. Did I believe in Heaven or not? Was this concept real or a figment of my imagination? Everyone around me assured me of Heaven's existence, and that my son was surely there, but was it true? I desperately needed to know. I needed to feel the truth, not just know it. And therein was my first problem.

2  C.S. Lewis, A Grief Observed, p. 25

Over the last few years, I have often said that I experienced a real disconnect between what I knew to be true *in my mind* and what I felt to be true *in my heart*. This mind/heart barrier was so painful to experience. On the one hand, I have studied the Bible continuously for nearly twenty-five years and believe it to be God's handbook for doctrine and living. On the other hand, my heart was so sorrowful that I felt no comfort because I couldn't actually experience Heaven while I still lived here on earth. In the words of C.S. Lewis again, "Only the locked door, the iron curtain, the vacuum, absolute zero."[3] What to do?

But then something curious happened. I began to study what Scripture said about Heaven, and found that there is so much contained in the pages of the Bible that was previously hidden from me until it "became a matter of life and death." Surprisingly, I realized that the only times I really "felt" the truths of Heaven were when I taught them to someone else, particularly to the wonderful, caring women of my church. Is it possible that convincing others of the comforts of Heaven brought me comfort as

---

3   C.S. Lewis, A Grief Observed, p. 7

well? Could it be that God really does reward those who diligently seek Him?[4]

So now you know my secret. This book is written by someone who has struggled with unbelief concerning the doctrine of Heaven. I am not completely healed of this, but am convinced that writing and teaching and sharing is the only way for me to make progress in this area.

My prayer has remained the same for these many months: "I believe, help my unbelief."[5] May God bless us all in this endeavor.

---

4   Hebrews 11:6
5   Mark 9:24

# What, No Harp?

The task of writing on the topic of Heaven is daunting. Where does one begin? What facets should be included? What do people really want to know? Is there a way to organize this material that is personal, approachable, and yet still true?

We *could* look to our culture for help. What do we find there? To some, of course, Heaven is all about floating on clouds while playing a harp. To others, Heaven is just one long, very boring worship service. The expectation of most is that nearly everyone will be in Heaven, except for those who commit heinous crimes against individuals and societies. Being reunited with loved ones is perhaps the universal hope of all who would believe in the afterlife. Only "very religious" people express interest in seeing God there. He really does seem to be just an afterthought for most people.

Our only recourse, and obviously the very best one, is to see and read and hear what the *Creator* of Heaven wishes to reveal to us about our eternal state. He has done this through the pages of Scripture. Why trust anyone else's opinion on this important matter? God created Heaven, He lives there, and He beckons us to be with Him. If we were planning on moving to Australia, we would not contact a friend in Germany who has never been there to find out what Australia is like. Surely God is the expert witness on Heaven who can and will reveal to us what we need to know about the future home that He has made for us.

"What no eye has seen, nor ear heard, nor the heart of man imagined . . . God has prepared for those who love Him."[6]

---

6   1 Corinthians 2:9

# A Very Good Place to Start

One of my favorite songs in one of my favorite movies (*The Sound of Music*) is "Do-Re-Mi." I enjoy this particular piece of music because it corresponds with how my mind works. Here is the opening verse:

> Let's start at the very beginning
> A very good place to start
> When you read you begin with A-B-C
> When you sing you begin with Do-Re-Mi

This logic (according to Maria) appeals to my sense of order. I need to learn things from the very beginning. I am not one who can jump into a subject in the middle of a lecture. I need to learn the basics of an area of interest before I can move on to more extensive study.

So it was with my thoughts of Heaven as I began to confront whether or not this doctrine could be of any help to me in my time of grief. Therefore, the first struggle was very foundational: Does Heaven really exist? Once I became convinced that Scripture overwhelmingly affirms the reality of a physical place called Heaven, I was then able to ask questions about actual life there. What do people do, day in and day out, for eternity? Next came this thought: Does knowing about the afterlife help me to live on this side of Heaven? And lastly, what about the Grand Finale of human history? Ephesians 1 states that God's goal is "to unite all things in Christ, things in heaven and things on earth."[7] What will this look like?

So let's start at the very beginning.

"In the beginning God created the *heavens* and the earth."[8]

---

7 Ephesians 1:10
8 Genesis 1:1

# Hints of Heaven?

"In the beginning, God created the heavens and the earth." Who says so? Well, God says so.[9] In these ten brief words, the opening verse of the Bible asserts that there is a heaven, there is an earth, and there is a God who made them both at the beginning of time. But if someone remains unconvinced of the absolute truth of the Scriptures, is there anything in the natural world that might speak to the existence of heaven?

Many are persuaded that the events that happen around us, to believers and unbelievers alike, point to the reality of something beyond this present life. For instance, how can we explain the experience of thousands of people throughout many centuries who claim that their bodies died, but that they had some additional existence in another realm for a time before they were brought back to their mortal lives on earth? Without evaluating the specifics of what people claim that other existence was like, we can at least observe that they indicate that life beyond this life was very real. Are *all* of these experiences to be dismissed as nothing?

Then there are some who believe that the seed germination process is a story that suggests new life after death. Here is the idea behind this one: Think

---

9   Genesis 1:1

about all the things that grow, and the seeds from which they come. They are planted in the earth, and somehow out of the "death" of a seed, a new life will begin. Beyond the specifics of how plants grow, there are other nature stories that whisper to us of life after death. A sunrise brings the glorious renewal of a new day, as does the beginning of spring every year. There seem to be countless messages throughout the course of our days on this earth that indicate that as one life dies away, a new life comes into being.

Other people use their reasoning powers to justify their belief in the existence of an "intelligent designer." How does one look at a beautiful sunset, or a new-born baby, or even the wonder of a single cell, and think that these have ultimately sprung out of nothingness? The proponents of this perspective would say that there must be an entity behind the world of creation, one who dwells in another sphere.

Finally (though this is not an exhaustive list!), some would argue that throughout the history of the world, people of all cultures and all faiths have believed in an afterlife. How do we explain this universality of focus on life beyond this earth?

So how would a skeptic crush all these hints suggesting the existence of an afterlife? Perhaps by saying that there is something within man that needs to explain away all the messiness of turmoil, grief, strife, illness, war, and other aspects of human existence. Man needs a crutch to survive life, and the supposed "hope" of heaven provides the much needed motivation for perseverance.

So do *you* find the above arguments from natural life persuasive? *My* answer? Thus far I tend to side with the skeptic.

# A New Heart

If we don't find substantial and convincing evidence from the natural world to prove the existence of Heaven, then where do we turn next? Is there any source that speaks to the previous examples that would confirm the reality of an afterlife? Of course there is: the Bible. Would this convince a skeptic? Only if God intervenes first.

God has to open our eyes, ears, and hearts to the Scriptures. Once we see, hear, and believe the truth about God and Heaven from the Bible, then we can look back at the whispers of life after death from nature or history and feel something of the hope of Heaven.

For example, let's return to the arguments from nature. Does the Bible see the seed germination process in any spiritual light? Both Jesus and Paul make extensive use of the lessons of nature that can be seen in this world in order to teach people about the life that cannot be seen. Both of them speak about a seed being planted as an analogy for our bodily death, and the life that somehow springs from that seed being a resurrection life.[10]

What about the fact that throughout history and across diverse cultures, men have set their hopes on

---

10  See John 12:23-26 and 1 Corinthians 15:35-38.

something beyond the grave? Ecclesiastes 3 addresses this: "God has put eternity into man's heart."[11]

How about "near-death" experiences? Jesus' friend Lazarus was in the grave for four days before Christ called him back to this world. Moses and Elijah appeared at the Transfiguration. Christ was seen by many eyewitnesses walking the earth after His crucifixion. John and Paul were both brought up into Heavenly places and then returned to earth in order to write of their experiences.

And finally, what about the beauty of the earth, the joy of a newborn baby, the amazing creation of a human cell? The Psalmist states: "When I look at your heavens, the work of your fingers, the moon and the stars, which you have set in place, what is man that you are mindful of him, and the son of man that you care for him?"[12]

Indeed, who am *I* that you are mindful of *me*? Why was I blessed to read your Word and then believe it? How is it that your Scriptures speak convincingly to my soul of the existence of Heaven?

Thank you, God, for taking the stone heart of a

---

11 Ecclesiastes 3:11
12 Psalm 8:3-4

skeptic and turning it into a heart of believing flesh.[13]

---

13  Ezekiel 36:26

# Shadowlands

There is much talk in the world of education about the "learning curve," which my dictionary defines as "the rate of a person's progress in gaining experience or new skills." Without going into too much detail, I would characterize myself as one with a learning curve problem. In college, I took Beginning Tennis at least three times (and I still couldn't hit a ball); and during Seminary a dear friend tried for two years to teach me how to sew (she ended up finishing all my projects).

So it was with reading and understanding the Bible. It wasn't until I was in my fourth church that I began to see Christ everywhere in the Old Testament. I had a very good pastor/teacher at that stage in my life, and he challenged me to go searching for Jesus in the pages of Scripture before His birth. This was a radical concept for me. I had always assumed that the Old Testament was everything that happened before the birth of Christ, and that the New Testament was the story of His life, death, and resurrection. What I didn't know was that Jesus can be discovered in every chapter of the Bible, all 1,189 of them!

So it was a similar situation with Heaven. I certainly knew that Jesus spoke a great deal about Heaven, that much of the New Testament testifies to the existence of Heaven, and that the book of

Revelation gives the most clues about what Heaven is like ("Neither shall there be mourning, nor crying, nor pain anymore"[14]). But the Old Testament? Outside of Genesis 1:1 ("In the beginning, God created the heavens and the earth"), I was oblivious to the massive amount of references to Heaven, until a new teacher came along to challenge me once again. The teacher this time? Grief.

Grief has a way of making one feel desperate—desperate to feel hope and joy again. Early in my journey I began to keep a Scripture journal. Basically I wrote out—long hand—any verse that touched my soul. I read the Bible much more slowly and carefully than ever before—because I certainly did not want to miss out on any reference to Heaven that I might skip over in my hurry to be healed. And the result? I was absolutely shocked at how much information there is in the Old Testament about Heaven.

Every chapter of the Bible, if considered rightly, has something to do with the eternal purpose of God. Heaven is a big part of that, for Ephesians 1 says that God will "unite all things in Christ, things in heaven and things on earth."[15] Is it reasonable to assume, then, that 78% of the Bible would be silent on the topic of Heaven?

14 Revelation 21:4
15 Ephesians 1:10

Unfortunately, I did think that—until I saw the Old Testament for what it was: a shadowland of beautiful Heavenly realities.

# Dreaming of Heaven

It took me a very long time to decide which of the 690 passages in the Bible that use the word "heaven" to write about next! There are just so many excellent ones that would help us all to understand more about the reality and existence of our future home. I narrowed down my search to one that was fascinating, one explained by Jesus Himself. That brought me to Genesis 28, the story of Jacob's dream:

> Jacob left Beersheba and went toward Haran. And he came to a certain place and stayed there that night, because the sun had set. Taking one of the stones of the place, he put it under his head and lay down in that place to sleep. And he dreamed, and behold, there was a ladder set up on the earth, and the top of it reached to heaven. And behold, the angels of God were ascending and descending on it! And behold, the Lord stood above it and said, "I am the Lord, the God of Abraham your father and the God of Isaac. The land on which you lie I will give to you and to your offspring. Your offspring shall be like the dust of the earth, and you

shall spread abroad to the west and to the east and to the north and to the south, and in you and your offspring shall all the families of the earth be blessed. Behold, I am with you and will keep you wherever you go, and will bring you back to this land. For I will not leave you until I have done what I have promised you." Then Jacob awoke from his sleep and said, "Surely the Lord is in this place, and I did not know it." And he was afraid and said, "How awesome is this place! This is none other than the house of God, and this is the gate of heaven."

What thrilled me so much about this particular passage is that I had never before really noticed the reference to "the gate of heaven." As a reminder, the gates of Eden were closed after the fall of our first parents, Adam and Eve. But here, just a few chapters later, it seems as though Jacob is actually seeing the gates of heaven. How delightful!

So what are the lessons to be learned in this passage? Certainly there are many, but our focus will be on the angels, the ladder, and the gate. More on these later. For now, consider the greatness of God in leaving us hints of heaven in this dream of

Jacob. The reality symbolized in his dream will be the key to opening the gates of heaven again.

# Heavenly Servants

We're in the beginning of studying Genesis 28, the episode of Jacob resting his head on a rock and dreaming of a ladder reaching into Heaven. First, of course, this passage affirms the reality of life beyond this earth, especially when understood properly. And it is easy to understand it properly, because Jesus Himself explains what it all means. That is the subject of the next chapter.

In the meantime, though, the passage contains a very interesting sentence about angels:

> And he dreamed, and behold, there was a ladder set up on the earth, and the top of it reached to heaven. And behold, the angels of God were ascending and descending on it![16]

Our culture, especially lately, seems to be very fascinated with angels. We see posters and books and music and calendars full of cherubic faces gazing up into the sky. But Genesis 28 doesn't match our cultural expectations. The angels in this verse seem to be very busy. But what are they doing?

---

16 Genesis 28:12

Matthew Henry (an 18th Century Bible Commentator) has a theory:

> Angels are employed as ministering spirits, to serve all the purposes and designs of Providence, and the wisdom of God is at the upper end of the ladder, directing all the motions of second causes to the glory of the first Cause. The angels are active spirits, continually ascending and descending; they rest not, day nor night, from service, according to the posts assigned them. They ascend, to give account of what they have done, and to receive orders; and then descend, to execute the orders they have received.[17]

This fits in well with Hebrews 1:14, which tells us that angels are "ministering spirits sent out to serve for the sake of those who are to inherit salvation." Some of the heirs of salvation are already at the top of Jacob's ladder, while some of us are left weeping here below. We know for sure that angels are servants to the heirs of salvation, working day and night for us, according to the express command of God.

17 Matthew Henry Online, Commentary on Genesis 28

28

I wonder how they serve our loved ones in Heaven above and what they are doing now in serving us here on earth?

# Can a Person Be a Ladder?

What is a ladder? One dictionary defines it as "an often portable structure consisting of two long sides crossed by parallel rungs, used to climb up and down." But have you ever heard the question "Who is a ladder?" Jesus has the answer, one that brings comfort to grieving souls.

The topic here refers to Jacob's dream in Genesis 28:

> Jacob left Beersheba and went toward Haran. And he came to a certain place and stayed there that night, because the sun had set. Taking one of the stones of the place, he put it under his head and lay down in that place to sleep. And he dreamed, and behold, there was a ladder set up on the earth, and the top of it reached to heaven. And behold, the angels of God were ascending and descending on it!

In a previous chapter we discussed the significance of the angels doing God's bidding by traveling between Heaven and Earth. But in John 1:51, Jesus makes an astounding statement, one that would surely not make Him any friends among the religious leaders of that time:

And he said to him, "Truly, truly, I say to you, you will see heaven opened, and the angels of God ascending and descending on the Son of Man."

Jesus was very clearly identifying Himself as the "ladder" between Heaven above and the earth below. Here is John Calvin's (Theologian and Pastor from the 16th Century) analysis of this remarkable answer to the question "Who is a ladder?"

It is Christ alone, therefore, who connects heaven and earth: he is the only Mediator who reaches from heaven down to earth: he is the medium through which the fullness of all celestial blessings flows down to us, and through which we, in turn, ascend to God. He it is who, being the head over angels, causes them to minister to his earthly members. Therefore (as we read in John 1:51), he properly claims for himself this honor, that after he shall have been manifested in the world, angels shall ascend and descend. If, then, we say that the ladder is a figure of Christ, the exposition will not be forced. For the similitude of a ladder well suits the Mediator, through whom ministering angels, righteousness and life, with all the graces of the Holy Spirit, descend to us step by step. We also, who were not only fixed to the earth, but plunged into the depths of the curse, and into hell itself, ascend even unto God. Also, the God of hosts is seated on the ladder; because the fullness of the Deity dwells in Christ; and hence also it is, that it reaches unto heaven.[18]

And what does all this have to do with helping those mourning the loss of a loved one? It is through the work of Jesus that we have the hope of seeing them again. Christ is a stable ladder between Heaven and earth. Anyone who dies in the Lord is safe in Him. That does not take away all our pain, but it does give us a secure hope, both for us and for our loved ones, that can never be taken away.

---

18 John Calvin Online, Commentary on Genesis 28

# The Closed Gate Reopened

> "Then Jacob awoke from his sleep and said, 'Surely the Lord is in this place, and I did not know it.' And he was afraid and said, 'How awesome is this place! This is none other than the house of God, and this is the gate of heaven.'"[19]

This is an intriguing end to a fascinating passage in Scripture. In the beginning of Genesis, we learned that the gate to Eden was closed off to Adam and Eve. And yet now, in His mercy and compassion, it seems as though God is opening it up again. Surely Jacob saw, with human eyes, the visible entrance into Heavenly realms.

What a joy to behold, and yet it caused Jacob to be afraid. This was not a fear based on perceived judgment, for God had just promised a wonderful future for Jacob and his offspring. Rather, it is a fear based on the incredible power and holiness and loving-kindness of God that enabled Jacob to see the open gate of Heaven.

Does it make you jealous of Jacob's experience? Wouldn't we all love to have a peek into Heaven? But yet I wonder if God hasn't given that to us

---

19 Genesis 28:16-17

already, and we're just not seeing it clearly. Isn't the very Word of God a window into His kingdom above? Aren't we privileged to participate in sacraments that mysteriously draw us closer into the presence of God? And what about worship itself?

We need to think about Jacob's dream whenever we enter into worship. The gathering of God's people is "none other than the house of God, and this the gate of heaven." That gate is opened to us when we worship God through Jesus Christ.

# Worshiping with Tears

Perhaps the most encouraging Scripture directly related to the loss of a loved one is found in 2 Samuel 12. It is the episode in which King David faces the pain of his son's death:

> But when David saw that his servants were whispering together, David understood that the child was dead. And David said to his servants, "Is the child dead?" They said, "He is dead." Then David arose from the earth and washed and anointed himself and changed his clothes. And he went into the house of the Lord and worshiped. He then went to his own house. And when he asked, they set food before him, and he ate. Then his servants said to him, "What is this thing that you have done? You fasted and wept for the child while he was alive; but when the child died, you arose and ate food." He said, "While the child was still alive, I fasted and wept, for I said, 'Who knows whether the Lord will be gracious to me, that the child may live?' But now he is dead. Why should I fast? Can I bring

him back again? I shall go to him,
but he will not return to me."

Two points are worthy of our consideration. The first is the astounding fact that David, when he heard of the passing of his son, chose to immediately enter the house of the Lord and worship. Perhaps he was just following the good example set by Job when he lost all his sons and daughters in a horrific act of providence:

> Then Job arose and tore his robe and shaved his head and fell on the ground and worshiped. And he said, "Naked I came from my mother's womb, and naked shall I return. The Lord gave, and the Lord has taken away; blessed be the name of the Lord."[20]

What courage! What faithfulness! What obedience! What amazing love that these two men, facing their darkest hour, chose to worship God. Scripture doesn't tell us how this was manifested—but it is reasonable to assume that both Job and David gave great thanks to God for their children.

And so we can do the same. While our initial reaction to the death of our loved ones might not have been one of immediate worship, we can surely

---

20 Job 1:20-21

begin even now. We can express to God our gratitude in allowing us even a short amount of time with the one who has been taken away from us.

They are so worth the pain that we are presently feeling, and though they will not come to us, one day we shall go to them.

# David's Comfort

There is one more observation that can be made concerning King David's reaction to the death of his infant son in 2 Samuel 12:

> "But now he is dead. Why should I fast? Can I bring him back again? I shall go to him, but he will not return to me."[21]

In this passage David first professes a statement of reality: His child was dead, and no amount of fasting or weeping could possibly bring him back to life. Death entered the world in Genesis 3 and has been wreaking havoc on this earth since then. Now it is David's turn to feel the effects of the Fall.

But David also expresses a profession of faith here: "I shall go to him." Is David saying that he would go to the grave one day, just as his child went to the grave? What kind of comfort would that be to anyone? The very next verse tells us that David comforted Bathsheba, the child's mother, after this sad loss. What comfort could David have given? He believed what he wrote in Psalm 23, that goodness and mercy would follow him all the days of his life, and that he would "dwell in the house of the Lord forever."

---

21  2 Samuel 12:23

David's infant son went to dwell in the house of the Lord forever. He would not return to David, but David knew that one day he would go to him in Heaven.

# Reduced to Rubble

In my limited training as grief counselor, I have read time and time again that we should resist the temptation to "rate" our griefs. All losses are awful, and it doesn't help to say to someone, "My sorrow is worse than yours!" As much as I agree with this principle, I think that the grief undergone by the biblical figure Job *really is* the worst one that we could imagine. Consequently, there are lessons to be learned from the way he dealt with his difficult circumstances, and it is to him that we now turn our attention.

The story is simple. Satan appears one day before God in Heaven. God asks him where he has been recently, and Satan replies that he has been traveling "to and fro" on the earth. God then asks Satan if he has noticed Job, a "blameless and upright man, who fears God and turns away from evil." Satan says that of course Job is good and fears God, because God has incredibly blessed him with family and friends and possessions. Satan argues that if those were removed, then Job would surely curse God. God then gives Satan permission to destroy seven sons, three daughters, and all his worldly goods. All these are taken away from Job, and his response is a famous one:

> And he said, "Naked I came from my mother's womb, and naked shall I

return. The Lord gave, and the Lord
has taken away: blessed be the name
of the Lord." In all this Job did not
sin or charge God with wrong.[22]

Apparently Satan is not pleased with this response
from Job and returns to God, challenging Him once
again:

Then Satan answered the Lord and
said, "Skin for skin! All that a man
has he will give for his life. But
stretch out your hand and touch his
bone and his flesh, and he will curse
you to your face."[23]

God assents to this, but with the condition that Job's
life be spared. Job is then afflicted with "loathsome
sores from the sole of his foot to the crown of his
head."[24]

This time even Job's wife is frustrated by her
husband's calm acceptance of all that has happened
to him:

Then his wife said to him, "Do you
still hold fast your integrity? Curse
God and die." But he said to her,

22 Job 1:21
23 Job 2:4-5
24 Job 2:7

"You speak as one of the foolish women would speak. Shall we receive good from God, and shall we not receive evil?" In all this Job did not sin with his lips.[25]

The first lesson to be learned here is that God is sovereign over Job and Satan alike. God is the shaper of all events, and Satan, while causing trouble for saints on earth, is only allowed to go so far in his mischief. God clearly has Satan on a leash. He cannot do anything without the permission of God. While this does not answer all of our questions about our losses or about how God rules from Heaven, we can take comfort in this: God is in charge. He does all things well, despite the grief and pain that we feel.

---

25  Job 2:9-10

# Wherein Lies the Hope?

Another lesson to be learned from studying the life and trials of Job pertains to guilt and regret. Next to immense feelings of sadness, my experience (both personally and in facilitating group discussions with other grievers) is that these two emotions are nearly universal. Everyone seems to have some area of doubt about what they could have done differently to possibly prolong the life of their loved one or to make the last interactions with them better. I have heard, "I should have noticed the symptoms earlier," or "We should have chosen a different doctor," or "I could have driven my daughter to the store instead of allowing her to take the car on her own," or "I wish I hadn't argued with my husband that morning." Such thoughts are traumatic and overwhelming, particularly in the early stages of grief. How can we escape such mental torture?

As mentioned before, Job underwent incredible suffering—loss of children, possessions, and health. The reader knows the story behind the story—that God had praised Job in the presence of Satan, and that Satan had challenged God to see if Job would still be faithful to Him if all were taken away. By the end of the book, we saw that Job aced the test and was greatly praised by God Himself. But in the midst of his pain and anguish, before everything was restored to him, he was still able to say: "The

Lord gave, and the Lord has taken away: blessed be the name of the Lord."[26]

Wherein lies the hope? For me it is in the realization that I don't know what has gone on in the Heavenly councils to bring about my present suffering. Like Job, I have not been made privy to the conversations that might have taken place. But I do know this: The Lord gives, and the Lord takes away. Blessed be the name of the Lord.

---

26 Job 1:21

# Long Before the Apostles Creed

While Job is most commonly remembered as someone who affirms the sovereignty and goodness of God even in the midst of severe trials, we must not miss his incredible faith as well. While dealing with the pain at the loss of his property, children, and health, and with miserable friends accusing him of bringing on this trial because of some yet un-confessed sin, Job makes one of the most astounding professions of faith in the resurrection and the reality of Heaven of anyone recorded in the Bible:

> Oh that my words were written!
>
> Oh that they were inscribed in a book!
>
> Oh that with an iron pen and lead they were engraved in the rock forever!
>
> For I know that my Redeemer lives, and at the last he will stand upon the earth.
>
> And after my skin has been thus destroyed,
>
> yet in my flesh I shall see God,

whom I shall see for myself,

and my eyes shall behold, and not
another.

My heart faints within me![27]

The ironic component of this verse is Job's wish
that he could write down all his words and all his
experiences. God certainly answered this desire in
an amazing way! Throughout the centuries
Christians have turned to this book of the Bible to
receive comfort from the Rock of Ages Himself.

But then Job turns to the main point of this passage,
and possibly the main point of the entire book. He
professes that "at the last" the Redeemer will return
to the earth. Long after Job has rested in the grave
he *knows* that he shall yet "in [his] flesh see God."
As if to affirm this point a second time, he
emphasizes that he "shall see for [himself], and
[his] eyes shall behold" God.

Long before there was an Apostles Creed, Job knew
in his mind and felt in his heart the last two phrases
that multitudes of believers have uttered countless
times: "I believe in the resurrection of the body; and
the life everlasting."

---

27 Job 19:23-27

All of our hearts should faint at the wonder of these truths!

# Heaven in the Psalms

Where does one begin to discuss all the references to Heaven in the book of Psalms? There are so many verses that speak directly about Heaven, while many others don't use that exact wording, but are still referring to life-after-life realities. There is suffering and grief and hope and glory present—sometimes even within the same Psalm!

To start us off, I skimmed through all 150 Psalms one day and wrote down only the references that used the word "Heaven." Here is a sampling:

> The Lord is in his holy temple; the Lord's throne is in heaven; his eyes see, his eyelids test, the children of man.[28]

> The Lord looks down from heaven on the children of man, to see if there are any who understand, who seek after God.[29]

> He will send from heaven and save me; he will put to shame him who tramples on me. God will send out his steadfast love and his

---

28 Psalms 11:4
29 Psalms 14:2

faithfulness![30]

O kingdoms of the earth, sing to God; sing praises to the Lord, to him who rides in the heavens, the ancient heavens; behold, he sends out his voice, his mighty voice.[31]

Turn again, O God of hosts! Look down from heaven, and see; have regard for this vine, the stock that your right hand planted, and for the son whom you made strong for yourself.[32]

For who in the skies can be compared to the Lord? Who among the heavenly beings is like the Lord, a God greatly to be feared in the council of the holy ones, and awesome above all who are around him?[33]

Let this be recorded for a generation to come, so that a people yet to be created may praise the Lord; that he looked down from his holy height;

---

30  Psalms 57:3
31  Psalms 68:23-33
32  Psalms 80:14-15
33  Psalms 89:6-7

from heaven the Lord looked at the earth, to hear the groans of the prisoners, to set free those who were doomed to die, that they may declare in Zion the name of the Lord, and in Jerusalem his praise, when peoples gather together, and kingdoms, to worship the Lord.[34]

Our God is in the heavens; he does all that he pleases.[35]

To you I lift up my eyes, O you who are enthroned in the heavens![36]

Give thanks to the God of heaven, for his steadfast love endures forever.[37]

Praise the Lord! Praise God in his sanctuary; praise him in his mighty heavens![38]

Even this cursory walk through the Psalms shows us how central heaven is to God. These poems and songs that the Lord gave for the worship of His Old

---

34 Psalms 102:18-22
35 Psalms 115:3
36 Psalms 123:1
37 Psalms 136:26
38 Psalms 150:1

Testament people prepare us for a life beyond this earth. God rules from that higher place. The Lord wants His people in all ages to live with an awareness of the blessing that is reserved for them even now in the heavens.

# Walking Through the Valley

No walk through the Bible on the subject of death or Heaven would be complete without a consideration of Psalm 23. This Psalm is perhaps the best known chapter in the entire Bible—to believers and unbelievers alike. It is quoted most often at funerals or in other situations where death is imminent. It provides assurance and comfort in the most difficult of times.

> The Lord is my shepherd; I shall not want.
>
> He makes me lie down in green pastures.
>
> He leads me beside still waters.
>
> He restores my soul.
>
> He leads me in paths of righteousness for his name's sake.
>
> Even though I walk through the valley of the shadow of death, I will fear no evil,
>
> for you are with me;

your rod and your staff, they comfort
me.

You prepare a table before me
in the presence of my enemies;

you anoint my head with oil;
my cup overflows.

Surely goodness and mercy shall
follow me all the days of my life,

and I shall dwell in the house of the
Lord forever.

For most people, and in most contexts, this Psalm is
particularly poignant and comforting when
contemplating one's own death. Very often this is
quoted to those facing a terminal illness or some
other end-of-life experience. At least, that's how I
looked at Psalm 23 until faced with the sudden
death of my son. Now, I have a different
perspective.

Those of us who have undergone the traumatic
death of a loved one feel that we are actually living
in the "valley of the shadow of death." In the
beginning, our loss pervades nearly every waking
moment. As time passes and we work through our
grief, the darkness lifts just a little. My own
personal experience, and those of others who have

walked this road before me, confirm that the valley can last for years. How can we survive such a long ordeal?

This Psalm helps us a great deal. We affirm that the Lord is our Shepherd. What do shepherds do? They are in charge of the flock every moment; they protect, shield, guide, and nourish the individual lambs. And that, of course, is what the Lord does for us.

We remind ourselves that we are to fear no evil because God's rod and staff are there for us. Despite our grief, we can live out the rest of our days with the assurance and confident expectation that at some point our cup will overflow again with many gifts of goodness and mercy from the hand of God. And best of all, we have the sure hope that we will dwell forever in the house of the Lord.

That's the kind of message we need to hear when the shadows around us seem so dark.

# Waiting

For those of us who grieve, there is a lot of time simply spent waiting. We wait for the present day to end, seeking relief in sleep. We wait for the crying and despair to give way to calm and peace once again. We wait for those "first" important events to be over: the birthday of our loved one, the anniversary of his death, the holiday season. We wait to see actual progress in our journey of grief, but it is too slow in coming. How will we ever survive the next twenty years (or more?) of our lives before we are reunited with our loved ones in Heaven? God's Word tells us how to survive these painfully long periods of waiting:

> Wait for the Lord; be strong, and let your heart take courage; wait for the Lord![39]

Oh, if only it were that simple! Our tendency is to feel just the opposite. We are certainly not strong, and our hearts are so broken that courage is not even on the radar screen. We are overcome with fear and weakness.

But this verse is not just a suggestion, it's a command. God instructs us in the way we should wait upon Him. In fact, the "wait for the Lord"

---

39 Psalm 27:14

phrases serve as the bookends to the "be strong and courageous" component of the verse. Why is waiting, with strength and courage, so important?

Paul Tripp helps us in our understanding of this concept in his book: *A Shelter in the Time of Storm: Meditations on God and Trouble*:

> For the child of God, waiting isn't simply about what the child will receive at the end of his wait. No, waiting is much more purposeful, efficient, and practical. Waiting is fundamentally about what we will become as we wait. God is using the wait to do in and through me exactly what He has promised. Through the wait He is changing me. By means of the wait He is altering the fabric of my thoughts and desires. Through the wait He is causing me to see and experience new things about Him and His kingdom. And all this sharpens me, enabling me to be a more useful tool in His redemptive hands.[40]

Not a single one of us would ever have volunteered to undergo grief and loss in order to be a useful tool in God's hands. Almost everyone living in this

40  Paul Tripp, A Shelter in the Time of Storm, p.143

fallen world will, at some point, have to deal with the sorrow that accompanies the death of a loved one. But given that reality, isn't it merciful of God to bring some *good* out of something really *awful*? Doesn't it help to know that we will be changed through this experience into more caring and compassionate people? Won't our eyes see the misery of others more clearly as a result of our own pain?

> Ye fearful saints, fresh courage take,
> The clouds ye so much dread
> Are big with mercy, and shall break
> In blessings on your head.[41]

So take the words of Psalm 27 as God's good command to you, a mercy in the midst of a cloud that you did not ask for: "Wait for the Lord; be strong, and let your heart take courage; wait for the Lord."

He is worth waiting for.

---

41  God Moves in a Mysterious Way, William Cowper

# Precious

There is a lovely verse in Psalm 116 which causes me to marvel about God's care for His people:

> Precious in the sight of the Lord is the death of His saints.[42]

How is the death of a saint "precious" to God? John Piper (Modern-day Pastor and Theologian), writing after the death of two good friends, explains:

> The death of every saint is a demonstration to all creation that Christ's atoning death was gloriously successful. It was not in vain. Therefore, the arrival of every saved saint in heaven is another trumpet-tribute to the preciousness of Christ's life and death on this earth. He must (it seems to me) take each one by the hand, as it were, and lead the saint to the Father, and say, "Look! Another trophy! Another 'fruit of my travail.' Another sinner saved and soul made perfect. O Father, look what we have wrought! Is this not precious!"[43]

---

42  Psalms 116:15
43  John Piper, Desiring God Blogpost, June 22, 1999.

*Precious in the sight of the Lord is the death of His saints.* God loves His people. When we think of our loved one's death, we, who are left behind, tend to focus on the details of how the person we miss so much left this world, and on the pain of life now without him. God, though, turns our attention to how he was welcomed into a better life beyond this one. From this perspective, the death of a saint can be a reminder of the Lord's special care for His children. He has a perfect life of future blessing prepared for each one of them.

God loves His saints more than we do. He proved this through the life and death of His own precious Son. Without the Cross and the reality of Heaven, we would not see our loved ones again, and their deaths could never be spoken of as something "precious."

# Seasons

Trivia question: What song from our popular musical heritage is entirely from the book of Ecclesiastes, except for six words written by the musician himself? If you guessed "Turn, Turn, Turn" you would be right! Pete Seeger wrote this hit in the 1950s. It was then popularized by the Byrds in a 1965 album of the same name. The only non-Scripture phrase which is sung is: "I swear it's not too late."

There are a few verses from the underlying Biblical text worth considering here on the topic of grieving and the hope of heaven:

> For everything there is a season, and a time for every matter under heaven: a time to be born, and a time to die . . . a time to weep, and a time to laugh . . . a time to mourn, and a time to dance.[44]

While these words make for a good song, they make for an even better commentary on life. There is no doubt that our lives "under the sun" are incredibly complex. The various emotions and life experiences described in this passage are dizzying to comprehend, especially while undergoing them. For

---

44 Ecclesiastes 3:1-4

instance, at the time when we are celebrating the joy of new life, we don't give a moment's thought to the reality that this adorable baby we are embracing will die one day. Or when we weep and mourn over the loss of someone very dear to us, we cannot imagine being able to laugh and dance once again. But these are realities that are common to nearly all of us. And if you are reading these words at all, it is probably because you have entered into a season of grief.

While death, weeping, and mourning are all sad events, one day we will be able to laugh and dance again. This earth and our troubled lives are ultimately in the control of Almighty God. Though we cannot always understand what He is doing, He is ruling over all things perfectly, and He loves us.

Therefore, we can trust Him in every season of our lives. One day He will take us beyond this world of "Turn, Turn, Turn," bringing us to an eternity of joy. Let the laughing and dancing begin even now, since God's promises to us can never fail.

# Wolves and Lambs

To be honest, I have lived my whole Christian life confused about the Prophetic books of the Bible. I never really understood this type of literature: the symbolism, the hyperbole, the nuanced language. This was the case until I faced grief. As often happens with God, His Word meets us where we are and takes us where we need to go. Now I find that Isaiah, Jeremiah, and the rest of the prophets comfort my heart with the anticipation of future Heavenly realities. It is to these writings that I now turn when I am in distress and in need of hope.

Isaiah contains numerous passages that are good examples of this new experience. There are so many gems here for those of us who mourn. While the Bible is sprinkled with *hints* of Heaven, Isaiah seems to abound with verses that cannot be interpreted in any other way than as *explicit* images of Heaven.

For instance, Isaiah 11:

> The wolf shall dwell with the lamb,
>
> and the leopard shall lie down with the young goat,
>
> and the calf and the lion and the fattened calf together;

and a little child shall lead them.

The cow and the bear shall graze;

their young shall lie down together;

and the lion shall eat straw like the ox.

The nursing child shall play over the hole of the cobra,

and the weaned child shall put his hand on the adder's den.

They shall not hurt or destroy in all my holy mountain;

for the earth shall be full of the knowledge of the Lord

as the waters cover the sea.[45]

Or Isaiah 25:

He will swallow up death forever; and the Lord God will wipe away tears from all faces, and the reproach of His people He will take away

---

45  Isaiah 11:6-9

from all the earth, for the Lord has spoken.[46]

How else can we explain these verses except that they are very clear promises of what is to come for God's people? There seems to be now no earthly possibility that wolves will dwell peacefully with lambs, that it would ever be safe for babies to play near cobras, or that death will die in our present lifetime.

But God will give us this and much more in Heaven. It is helpful for those of us struggling with grief to read these passages, to consider, to dream, and to believe.

---

46 Isaiah 25:8

# Singing for Joy

Isaiah 49 contains a beautiful passage that has meant a great deal to me personally. It brings me comfort because it displays the great character of God. I hope it will do the same for you.

> Sing for joy, O heavens, and exult, O earth;
>
> break forth, O mountains, into singing!
>
> For the Lord has comforted his people
>
> and will have compassion on his afflicted.
>
> But Zion said, "The Lord has forsaken me;
>
> my Lord has forgotten me."[47]

At first glance, the opening of this passage seems strangely out of place for what follows. The context, though, explains the exuberance that is contained here. Immediately prior to this God encourages the Israelites to persevere in the midst of a very difficult

---

47 Isaiah 49:13-14

struggle, the upcoming exile. God is very clear that His intent is to restore Israel someday. Until that time His people need to remember all His promises, especially when they become tempted to believe that God has forsaken them. Don't grieving souls need this help as well?

John Calvin explains it in this way:

> Afflictions trouble our consciences, and cause them to waver in such a manner that it is not so easy to rest firmly on the promises of God. In short, men either remain in suspense, or tremble, or utterly fall and even faint. So long as they are oppressed by fear or anxiety, or grief, they scarcely accept of any consolation; and therefore they need to be confirmed in various ways. This is the reason why Isaiah describes the advantages of this deliverance in such lofty terms, in order that believers, though they beheld nothing around them but death and ruin, might sustain their heart by the hope of a better condition. Accordingly, he places the subject almost before their eye, that they may be fully convinced that they shall have the most abundant cause

of rejoicing; though at that time they saw nothing but grief and sorrow.[48]

These truths are for us, also. Whenever we are overwhelmed by fear, anxiety, or grief, we need to turn to the One who makes great promises and then keeps them. God will never leave us or forsake us. He will comfort His people and have compassion on those who are afflicted. One day we will be delivered from the oppression of our sorrow. One day we shall be transported to a much better condition—Heaven itself. And one day we will sing for joy.

---

48  John Calvin Online, Commentary on Isaiah 49

# The Palms of His Hands

The second half of that passage in Isaiah 49 is just as amazing as the first. We see a strong promise early on that the God of the universe will have compassion on His people; but these later verses also describe God in very human terms:

> Can a woman forget her nursing child,
>
> that she should have no compassion on the son of her womb?
>
> Even these may forget,
>
> yet I will not forget you.
>
> Behold, I have engraved you on the palms of my hands.[49]

In the midst of grief and sorrow, it is so easy to feel abandoned by God. But God assures us here that even if a human mother could turn away from her hurting child, God cannot. And to prove His great love and care for us, He has gone so far as to engrave our names on the palms of His hands. Oh, that we could truly envision this—it would give us a new appreciation of the endless depths of His

---

49 Isaiah 49:15-16a

compassion.

Does He have anything else on the palms of His hands, besides our names? Yes, He does. He has the visible marks of the nails that were hammered in during His crucifixion. Is that not proof enough of His everlasting love?

May we always look to His hands whenever we are tempted to believe that He has forgotten us.

# Lamentations

What better place to turn in the Bible to help a grieving soul than the book of Lamentations? The actual name of this book originated from the Latin word *lamentationem*, meaning "wailing, moaning, weeping." Jeremiah wrote this part of Scripture to describe the desolation of Judah after the fall of Jerusalem in 586 BC, but there are many verses that are particularly appropriate for those of us sorrowing over the loss of a loved one.

Here is one such section:

> [God] has filled me with bitterness; he has sated me with wormwood. He has made my teeth grind on gravel, and made me cower in ashes; my soul is bereft of peace; I have forgotten what happiness is; so I say, "My endurance has perished; so has my hope from the Lord."[50]

Isn't this an apt description of grief? Lacking peace, forgetting what happiness is, flagging endurance, and hopelessness?

Jeremiah continues:

---

50 Lamentations 3:15-18

Remember my affliction and my
wanderings, the wormwood and the
gall! My soul continually remembers
it and is bowed down within me.[51]

This prayer is directed to God that He would
remember the many trials that have been already
endured. Asking this causes Jeremiah's soul, the
very core of his physical, mental, and spiritual
being, to bow down in humility, reverence, and
submission to God's sovereignty and providence in
the midst of such anguish.

The tone of the next verse, though, changes
dramatically:

But this I call to mind, and therefore
I have hope: The steadfast love of
the Lord never ceases; his mercies
never come to an end; they are new
every morning; great is your
faithfulness. "The Lord is my
portion," says my soul, "therefore I
will hope in him."[52]

Reminding God of His actions reminds the one
praying of a few things as well: God will never

---

51 Lamentations 3:19-20
52 Lamentations 3:21-24

forget or forsake us, and He brings new kindnesses to us each and every day.

When we are engulfed by feelings of despair, there really is no better remedy than to recount the mercies of God. It is no small matter to "count your blessings, one by one." Doing so causes us to remember the faithfulness of God even when we are overcome by lamentation. Each morning we need to wait in confident expectation to see how God's love and compassion will be revealed to us during the course of the day.

God is the source of our hope. When everything else fails, He alone remains faithful.

# Jumping for Joy

Can grief co-exist with joy? What about pain with contentment? Do our afflictions still allow us to have a sense of personal peace? These are difficult questions to ponder, especially in the midst of great turmoil and sorrow. The Bible, though, seems to suggest that the answer is "yes" to all these questions.

One passage that helps us reach that conclusion is found in Habakkuk:

> Though the fig tree should not blossom,
>
> nor fruit be on the vines,
>
> the produce of the olive fail
>
> and the fields yield no food,
>
> the flock be cut off from the fold
>
> and there be no herd in the stalls,
>
> yet I will rejoice in the Lord;
>
> I will take joy in the God of my salvation.

God, the Lord, is my strength;

he makes my feet like the deer's;

he makes me tread on my high places.[53]

We must remember that the prophet Habukkuk wrote to a very agrarian society—and so he used the language of vines and flocks. A modern day rendering of this Scripture would surely include words that we would be much more familiar with. But the essence of the passage is the same— yesterday, today, and tomorrow.

Sometimes God takes from us what we cherish the most. Most likely that is the reason you are reading this; you have lost someone very close and dear to your heart. In the early years of grief, it seems incomprehensible that joy, contentment, and peace will ever return as common emotions in our lives. But shouldn't they? Isn't it possible that grief, pain, and affliction will one day subside enough to allow positive emotions to surface once again?

Here is what Matthew Henry has to say regarding these verses in Habakkuk:

> But those who, when they were full, enjoyed God in all, when they are

53  Habakkuk 3:17-19

emptied and impoverished can enjoy all in God, and can sit down upon a melancholy heap of the ruins of all their creature comforts and even then can sing to the praise and glory of God, as the God of their salvation. This is the principal ground of our joy in God, that he is the God of our salvation, our eternal salvation, the salvation of the soul; and, if he be so, we may rejoice in him as such in our greatest distresses, since by them our salvation cannot be hindered, but may be furthered. Note, Joy in God is never out of season, nay, it is in a special manner seasonable when we meet with losses and crosses in the world, that it may then appear that our hearts are not set upon these things, nor our happiness bound up in them. See how the prophet triumphs in God: The Lord God is my strength, v. 19. He that is the God of our salvation in another world will be our strength in this world, to carry us on in our journey thither, and help us over the difficulties and oppositions we meet with in our way.[54]

---

54 Matthew Henry Online, Commentary on Habakkuk

If eternal salvation has been secured for us, then we *can* experience joy in the midst of our grief. We *can* feel pain and yet be contented in the reality of our future existence. And we *can* be filled with the peace that passes all understanding even when we are afflicted with great difficulties.

We must learn to trust God and not our circumstances. The God of our salvation will indeed be our strength, both in this life and in the life to come.

# What Would Jesus Say?

Our journey through the Scriptures on the topic of Heaven is about to change rather dramatically. And why is that? It's because we are, for the moment, finished with the Old Testament and moving on to the New. While there are numerous other Old Testament verses that could be used for our comfort, perhaps it's best that we now enter into the realm of the Gospel accounts of Matthew, Mark, Luke, and John.

Throughout our entire previous discussion of the Old Testament, we are left with the nagging desire to "interview" someone who has been to Heaven and back. Can you imagine the questions we might ask, or the insights that might be shared? If only we had something more than shadows and visions to hold onto while we face the dark night of our grief. . . . Actually, we do!

The word "Gospel" literally means "Good News." And the Good News for us is that the Gospels contain the words, insights, and descriptions of One who *has* been to Heaven and is willing to tell us first-hand accounts of what awaits us! Of course this traveler is Jesus Christ. Here is His own testimony:

> I came from the Father and have come into the world, and now I am

leaving the world and going to the
Father.[55]

What better person to help us in our grief than the
one who has been a citizen and resident of Heaven
for as long as Heaven has existed? Who has a more
credible testimony than Jesus concerning the
realities of life beyond death? And why shouldn't
we study and reflect upon the promises of
everlasting bliss that come to us from the premiere
expert witness on this important topic?

What a blessing to have authoritative words about
Heaven from the Person who knows it so well!

---

55 John 16:28

# Blessed

Undergoing a tragic loss in one's life certainly changes the definition of the phrase "blessing from God." In the years since losing my son, I have found myself very much troubled by those who say (in person or in emails, Christmas cards, Facebook statuses, etc.) something like this: "My life is great. My kids are great. My job is great. My family is great. God is really blessing me!"

Now before I hear protests of "You are just jealous!" let me explain that in no way am I disputing the idea that God blesses us with wonderful gifts of family harmony, job satisfaction, and physical and spiritual growth of children. I truly do rejoice in how God blesses His people.

But at the same time, I also have this nagging question: "Hmm. If God is blessing this person with all these happy providences, does this mean God is *not* blessing me in my loss? Am I experiencing an anti-blessing? What about me, God? I want to be blessed, too!"

See the dilemma? Thankfully, Jesus Himself answers this question directly in the Sermon on the Mount, found in Matthew 5:

> Seeing the crowds, he went up on the
> mountain, and when he sat down, his

disciples came to him. And he opened his mouth and taught them, saying: "Blessed are the poor in spirit, for theirs is the kingdom of heaven. Blessed are those who mourn, for they shall be comforted."[56]

Anyone who has suffered the loss of a precious friend knows the feeling of being "poor in spirit." Anyone who has cried repeatedly because of missing the love of a relative understands "mourning." So what does Jesus mean that we are "blessed?"

It doesn't mean that we should be rejoicing or happy with the event which led to the grieving process, but it does demonstrate that God has a blessing for us in the midst of this difficult period in our lives. Being "poor in spirit" shows a dependence upon God and His mercies which perhaps we hadn't really felt before; and "mourning" causes us to seek healing, forgiveness, and compassion from the only One who could possibly help us.

With loss can come humility, and God gives grace to the humble.[57] He will not despise a broken and

---

56 Matthew 5:1-4
57 James 4:6

contrite heart.[58] But more than anything else that we have here and now, those who are poor in spirit and who are mourning are taught by suffering and grace to wait for the fullness of comfort that will be ours in the kingdom of Heaven.

58 Psalms 51:17

# His Eye Is on the Sparrow

The following passage may at first seem like an odd place to find Heavenly comfort following the death of someone dear to us. But comparing ourselves to birds may be very helpful, as it turns out, if Jesus is the one who is drawing our attention to them.

> Are not two sparrows sold for a penny? And not one of them will fall to the ground apart from your Father. But even the hairs of your head are all numbered. Fear not, therefore; you are of more value than many sparrows.[59]

This passage addresses the greater issue of fear—which is certainly no stranger to those who have lost someone close. We fear the pathway of sorrow, both for ourselves and others who are mourning; we fear that another dear one might be taken from us; we fear for the eternal state of the one we've just lost. Widows fear loneliness and lack of protection now that their husbands are gone; grieving parents fear the future without the child who could have cared for them in their old age, and they accuse themselves, wondering if they could have done more to save their children from death. Nearly every death results, at least for a time, in anxious

---

59 Matthew 10:29-31

thoughts.

So how do sparrows help? Jesus pronounces in these verses that sparrows are watched by God every moment of every day. Given that we, children of the living God, are of "more value than many sparrows," Jesus is emphatically stating that not even a hair can fall from our heads without His notice. Imagine that!

This passage helps us to understand that the death of our loved one did not surprise God. He more than noticed this tragic event. He sees our tears and comforts us in the way that only He can. He hears our fearful thoughts and encourages us to persevere on our journey of grief. He supplies all the grace and mercy necessary to carry us forward. God even gives us the energy and love to reach out to others who suffer loss.

Let's fight our fear with these words of Jesus. The next time we see a sparrow, let's give a smile (feeble though it may be) and a prayer of thanksgiving to God for His immeasurable goodness to us in orchestrating all events, even painful ones, for our good and His glory.

# Will We Know One Another?

There are two questions that seem to arise constantly in the minds of those who have lost a loved one. The first involves whether or not we will know one another in Heaven, the other is whether or not we will still be married to our spouses in Heaven. The second of these will be addressed soon, but the first question will be explored now and in the next section as well.

One of the clearest indications that we will indeed recognize one another in Heaven comes from Matthew 17, the account of the Transfiguration of Christ:

> And after six days Jesus took with him Peter and James, and John his brother, and led them up a high mountain by themselves. And he was transfigured before them, and his face shone like the sun, and his clothes became white as light. And behold, there appeared to them Moses and Elijah, talking with him.[60]

The dictionary definition of transfiguration is this: "A complete change of form or appearance into a more beautiful or spiritual state." At first glance,

---

60  Matthew 17:1-3

then, it would appear that perhaps we will not know one another, if it involves a complete change of appearance. However, it is also apparent that Peter, James, and John recognized Jesus, Moses, and Elijah, even though the last three were "transfigured." This is quite remarkable since obviously Peter, James, and John had never personally met Moses and Elijah, since those men lived on earth many centuries before this incident took place.

While it is not wise to speculate too much on what is not said directly in Scripture, I do believe that this passage suggests that we will know one another in glory. We will not be hindered by the "more beautiful or spiritual state" of one another; in fact, it will be a true delight to see one another "perfected."

If the disciples knew people they had never met before when they saw them at the Transfiguration, it would seem very strange for us to be unable to recognize people in Heaven whom we have known very well on earth. In fact, this passage seems to imply that we will even be able to recognize many people in eternity that we have never met before, people like Moses and Elijah.

How amazing is that?

# Please Send Someone!

As if wondering whether we will know one another in Heaven isn't big enough to wrap our brains around, how about this: Will those in Heaven be able to speak with those in Hell? Yikes! Here is a passage of Scripture which will either clarify our thoughts or confuse us even more in answering this question:

> There was a rich man who was clothed in purple and fine linen and who feasted sumptuously every day. And at his gate was laid a poor man named Lazarus, covered with sores, who desired to be fed with what fell from the rich man's table. Moreover, even the dogs came and licked his sores. The poor man died and was carried by the angels to Abraham's side. The rich man also died and was buried, and in Hades, being in torment, he lifted up his eyes and saw Abraham far off and Lazarus at his side. And he called out, "Father Abraham, have mercy on me, and send Lazarus to dip the end of his finger in water and cool my tongue, for I am in anguish in this flame." But Abraham said, "Child, remember that you in your lifetime received

your good things, and Lazarus in like manner bad things; but now he is comforted here, and you are in anguish. And besides all this, between us and you a great chasm has been fixed, in order that those who would pass from here to you may not be able, and none may cross from there to us." And he said, "Then I beg you, father, to send him to my father's house—for I have five brothers—so that he may warn them, lest they also come into this place of torment." But Abraham said, "They have Moses and the Prophets; let them hear them." And he said, "No, father Abraham, but if someone goes to them from the dead, they will repent." He said to him, "If they do not hear Moses and the Prophets, neither will they be convinced if someone should rise from the dead."[61]

These verses describe a conversation between someone in Hell and someone in Heaven. So what can we learn from this story?

1. Jesus wants us to know that there is a Heaven and a Hell.

---

61 Luke 16

2. At least in this passage, a man in Heaven and a man in Hell are interacting with each other.

3. Life after death does not mean the loss of personal history and memory. The rich man remembers his life on earth and knows very well who Lazarus is.

4. The rich ruler still thinks Lazarus should be his errand boy. He wants him to bring water to Hell, and then later he wants to send Lazarus back to earth.

5. The rich man is concerned with the fate of his brothers, not wanting them to end up in Hell as he has. His solution is to send someone who has died back to earth to encourage them to repent.

6. There is no second chance after death. We need to repent now.

7. Jesus *did* come back from the dead, telling us that Heaven and Hell are real. Let's be sure that we listen to what He says.

# Together Forever?

There is one sentence in the New Testament that has caused much anguish and heartache to those who have lost spouses to death.

> And Jesus said to them, "The sons of this age marry and are given in marriage, but those who are considered worthy to attain to that age and to the resurrection from the dead neither marry nor are given in marriage, or they cannot die anymore, because they are equal to angels and are sons of God, being sons of the resurrection."[62]

Jesus is making a point about two different eras of time: now on earth and later in Heaven. Many lament that they will no longer be "married" in Heaven, but if one looks closely at this passage, it is stating that there will be no "weddings" in the age to come. Marriage is a holy ordinance provided by God from the beginning of time that according to His direction a "man should leave his father and mother and be joined to his wife, and they shall become one flesh."[63] One of the main purposes of marriage is the procreation of children, and it is

---

62 Luke 20:34-36
63 Genesis 2:24

clear that such an activity will be not be taking place after our lives are completed here on earth. So "marriage," in this sense, will not be necessary.

However, we don't have to insist, as some do, that those who are married here on earth will not be especially close to one another when reunited in Heaven. Jesus is not saying that our spouses will be irrelevant to us in our new lives in Heaven. If the rich man could remember his dealings with Lazarus, how could it be that husbands and wives would forget their special love for one another? Why would we think that God will not enrich our experience in Heaven through our reunion with special people? It seems unlikely that we will be in Heaven saying "This is great, but I just wish I could see my husband of fifty-five years."

Better to trust that your husband or wife will be special to you in Heaven, with the greater promise that "they cannot die anymore." And praise God that because of the Father's electing love, Christ's atoning work on the Cross, and the pouring out of the Holy Spirit upon our hearts, we will forever be sons and daughters of the resurrection, and the bride of Christ, our Husband.

And that is one wedding that we will all attend!

# The Tears of Jesus

It's pretty amazing that the shortest verse in the Bible is perhaps the best one for comforting those who are grieving the loss of a loved one. It occurs in John 11, as Jesus stands outside the tomb of his good friend Lazarus, who died four days before His arrival.

Jesus wept.[64]

What makes these two words so remarkable? It's that Christ knew that He would raise Lazarus from the dead in just a few moments, and yet He still shed tears. He was sad that Lazarus had died, and sad that his family and friends were grieving:

> When Jesus saw [Mary] weeping,
> and the Jews who had come with her
> also weeping, he was deeply moved
> in his spirit and greatly troubled.[65]

What a compassionate Lord and Savior to grieve Himself at the loss of someone He loved. It says much about His dual nature, being Man and God, that He would cry in His humanity before resurrecting Lazarus in His divinity.

---

64  John 11:35
65  John 11:33

What benefit is this short verse to us? If ever we've been told that we should "just get over" our grief, or that if we were stronger in our faith we'd be able to stop crying, this passage would carry us through. No one would dare accuse Jesus of being too emotionally or spiritually weak. The fact that Jesus experienced the same emotions of mourning that we do should be of great comfort to us—we have a God who understands that death is the enemy, that losing a loved one hurts, and that our spirits will be greatly troubled by the grief and despair of those around us.

But even greater is the fact that Jesus has the power to reverse the awful reality of death, and will do for our loved ones what He did for Lazarus: raise them from their graves. He not only feels our pain, but does something about it.

Let's look through our tears to the One who will wipe them away someday, while praising God today for His sympathy toward us. Our losses matter to God, and thankfully He has created Heaven as a place where everything that is so badly broken now will be made finally and perfectly whole.

# What's in a Name?

It should come as no surprise to believers that the words of Jesus bring great comfort to a grieving soul. When we experience great sorrow, we need to know that He notices our tears. Psalm 56:8 actually affirms that God has "put my tears in [his] bottle." God keeps count of our every tear. What an amazing, personal God we serve.

But there is an even clearer incident in the life of Jesus to demonstrate how He knows each one of us by name. It occurs on the day of His resurrection. Mary, one of the faithful women who cared for Him in life and death, arrives at the tomb to anoint His body with spices.

> And she saw two angels in white, sitting where the body of Jesus had lain, one at the head and one at the feet. They said to her, "Woman, why are you weeping?" She said to them, "They have taken away my Lord, and I do not know where they have laid him." Having said this, she turned around and saw Jesus standing, but she did not know that it was Jesus. Jesus said to her, "Woman, why are you weeping? Whom are you seeking?" Supposing him to be the gardener, she said to

him, "Sir, if you have carried him away, tell me where you have laid him, and I will take him away." Jesus said to her, "Mary." She turned and said to him in Aramaic, "*Rabboni!*" (which means Teacher).[66]

Isn't this lovely? Through her tears Mary was unable to recognize the one whom she was seeking, until He uttered a simple word: "Mary." Immediately she recognized Him and was able to then respond to Him in a similar way: "Teacher."

We should respond in a like manner. We should ask ourselves, "Why are we weeping?" when the Creator of the Heavens and the Earth is waiting for us to recognize His voice through the Scriptures. "The sheep hear his voice, and he calls his own sheep by name and leads them out . . . for they know his voice."[67]

So the next time you are overwhelmed with distress and grief, imagine yourself in the presence of your Lord as He comforts you with this one word: your name.

---

66  John 20:12-16
67  John 10:3-4

# The Future

In the midst of our darkest grief, it is hard to imagine anything being worthwhile to anticipate. Even the most joyous future events seem incredibly painful to us. Imagine a brother's wedding and his sister is not in attendance. Or a woman meeting her first grandchild in the delivery room without her husband—the baby's grandfather. Any scenario would work here—imagine your own circumstance. Most of us have only flippantly used the word "bittersweet" in the past, but now we truly understand the meaning. Try as we might, it is difficult to rejoice in future joyous events.

But we must do just that. Why? Because God calls us to do so. In Romans 8 we are confronted with a seemingly impossible task: to happily consider what lies ahead of us:

> For I consider that the sufferings of
> this present time are not worth
> comparing with the glory that is to
> be revealed to us.[68]

Since my son's death I have often commented on the dichotomy between my head and my heart. Although these two organs within my body are not very far from one another, in reality they are worlds

---

68 Romans 8:18

apart. What I feel is often in conflict with what I know, and what I know rebels against my feelings. Perhaps God, knowing our frailty, gives us passages like this one to lead us toward healing. We must meditate continually upon the promises of God to calm our feelings of sorrow and despair.

Matthew Henry has an interesting commentary on this verse, beginning with the obvious statement that Paul, of all people, was personally acquainted with suffering, but also with future glory:

> Now Paul was as competent a judge of this point as ever any mere man was. He could reckon not by art only, but by experience; for he knew both. He knew what the sufferings of this present time were; He knew what the glory of heaven is. And, upon the view of both, he gives this judgment here. There is nothing like a believing view of the glory which shall be revealed to support and bear up the spirit under all the sufferings of this present time. . . . As the saints are suffering, so they are waiting. Heaven is therefore sure; for God by his Spirit would not raise and encourage those hopes only to defeat and disappoint them. He will establish that word unto his servants

on which he has caused them to hope (Psalms 119:49), and heaven is therefore sweet; for, if hope deferred makes the heart sick, surely when the desire comes it will be a tree of life (Prov. 13:12).[69]

Experience has shown you what your present suffering is. Through faith and the Word of God, however, you can hold on to what your future glory shall be. One day there will no longer be any event that is bittersweet; in fact, bitterness will be eliminated from our vocabulary and from our lives.

Let's ask God to enlighten our hearts to the glorious truths of Heaven, where our eternal future will be forever as wonderful as our eternal present.

---

69 Matthew Henry Online, Commentary on Romans 8

# The Death of Death

I once saw a passage of Scripture on the door leading into the nursery at a local church: "We shall not all sleep, but we shall all be changed." While this is a creative and humorous sign regarding the care of children, it is also a wonderful help to those struggling with loss and bereavement. It is found in 1 Corinthians 15, and is part of a beautiful description of the great reality that awaits us someday.

In fact, this entire chapter of the Bible is devoted solely to Paul's thoughts and reflections on the doctrine of the resurrection. It would take weeks to unpack the insights that this one chapter gives to us, but a few highlights will have to suffice for now.

Paul reminds us early on what he considers to be crucial information for us:

> For I delivered to you as of first importance what I also received: that Christ died for our sins in accordance with the Scriptures, that he was buried, that he was raised on the third day in accordance with the Scriptures, and that he appeared to Cephas, then to the twelve. Then he appeared to more than five hundred brothers at one time, most of whom

are still alive, though some have
fallen asleep.[70]

Why is Christ's resurrection "of first importance" to
those of us who are mourning the loss of someone
dear? Because without it, nothing else matters.
There is no hope of any meaning to life if Christ did
not show Himself to the world after His death on
the cross. As Paul so correctly states in the
nineteenth verse, without His resurrection,
Christians "are of all people most to be pitied."
Faith is pointless without Christ's resurrection. If
the historical account of Christ's rising from the
dead is not to be trusted, then there is no way we
can ever hope for our own resurrection. We are then
left with an Ecclesiastes kind of moment: What's
the point of living and dying? Is our existence and
suffering just some cosmic bad luck?

Ah, but the good news of Christ's resurrection
reigns over all the skepticism and doubt that anyone
of us can experience, and it is a truth to be
embraced and celebrated:

> Behold! I tell you a mystery. We
> shall not all sleep, but we shall all be
> changed, in a moment, in the
> twinkling of an eye, at the last
> trumpet. For the trumpet will sound,
> and the dead will be raised

70  1 Corinthians 15:3

imperishable, and we shall be changed. For this perishable body must put on the imperishable, and this mortal body must put on immortality. When the perishable puts on the imperishable, and the mortal puts on immortality, then shall come to pass the saying that is written:

Death is swallowed up in victory.
O death, where is your victory?
O death, where is your sting?

The sting of death is sin, and the power of sin is the law. But thanks be to God, who gives us the victory through our Lord Jesus Christ.[71]

As we fight despair and depression after the death of a friend or relative, let's remember what is of first importance. Because of God's incredible mercy to us, we will one day celebrate the victory of Christ over death. We will be granted the privilege of witnessing the ultimate irony: the death of death. And none of us will cry at that funeral.

---

71  1 Corinthians 15:51-55

# Comfort One Another

At some point on our journey of grief, we will begin to feel better. This healing will certainly be experienced in different ways and at different times for different people. Some of us will not cry as much, angry thoughts might disappear, others will be able to laugh again, and some will even find that the memories of their loved one have become more sweet than bitter. We might even begin to give comfort to others in their loss. This seems to be God's design for grieving people:

> Blessed be the God and Father of our Lord Jesus Christ, the Father of mercies and God of all comfort, who comforts us in all our affliction, so that we may be able to comfort those who are in any affliction, with the comfort with which we ourselves are comforted by God.[72]

As God comforts us, we are to comfort others. Paul Tripp states that we who have been confronted with death and then comforted by God should not become just "containers of comfort, but conduits of comfort."[73] As we experience the healing that comes from God alone, we should look around at the

---

72  2 Corinthians 1:3-4
73  Paul Tripp, Interview on GriefShare DVD

misery in this world and attempt to alleviate the sufferings of others with the comfort we have received. As weak as we may feel, Jesus calls upon us to minister His comfort to others. This is all so mysterious to us, but God has ordained that frail people are to be His healing hands to a hurting world.

And how is this done? A few verses after the above passage, Paul recounts some of his own afflictions, and states that this was God's purpose for them: "That was to make us rely not on ourselves but on God who raises the dead."[74]

Isn't this the greatest comfort that we can give others who are feeling pain and misery? We can attest to the fact that in our own despair, we have learned not to rely on ourselves (Have we been able to help ourselves? Probably not.) but on God alone who freely and generously relieves our sorrows and burdens. He is the Father of mercies and the God of all comfort.

The ultimate encouragement, of course, is that God will raise the dead. Those who have died and gone before us will one day welcome us into the gates of Heaven. Blessed be the God and Father of our Lord Jesus Christ.

Be still, my soul: the hour is hast'ning on

---

74 2 Corinthians 1:9

When we shall be forever with the Lord,
When disappointment, grief, and fear are gone,
Sorrow forgot, love's purest joys restored.
Be still, my soul: when change and tears are past,
all safe and blessed we shall meet at last.[75]

---

75 Be Still My Soul, Katharina von Schlegel

# A Shining Lamp

Ask any Christian when they became really knowledgeable of the doctrine of Heaven, and I'd bet it would be *after* the death of a loved one. There is something of the desperation of a grieving soul that needs to grasp the reality of where loved ones have gone that propels the searching of Scripture verses to help ease the pain. Certainly that was the case with me; as stated in the introduction, this book is a result of my own frantic need to understand the realities of life after death.

And what did I find? That God is most gracious to give us information that will indeed aid in our healing. Sometimes it comes in a very small verse, like Philippians 1:21: "For to me to live is Christ, and to die is gain." Thanks be to God that He informs us that being with Him in Heaven is better than life here on earth, as wonderful as life in this world may be. Consider all the best of life experiences here below: precious relationships, the beauty of creation, the joy of new life, etc. But Paul is stating that "to die is gain." What an encouraging thought.

Or sometimes God through Scripture gives us a whole new way of looking at the big picture of life, as in Philippians 3:20: "But our citizenship is in Heaven." Any rumblings of homesickness for an unseen place of glory that we feel here on earth are understandable in light of this passage—we were not destined to be comfortable in this present life because we are not *home* yet. Our true home is in Heaven, where we will experience all the privileges of real citizenship, including freedom from sin, death, and pain.

But we are also encouraged to stand firm in the midst of suffering and grief while we live on this side of Heaven: "Now may our Lord Jesus Christ himself, and God our Father, who loved us and gave us eternal comfort and good hope through grace, comfort your hearts and establish them in every good work and word."[76] It certainly sounds as though God has already given us this "eternal comfort and good hope." Somehow we need to grasp hold of these eternal concepts in order to be equipped to do good works and to give words of comfort to others now.

We need to praise God for all these morsels of Heavenly truths that He distributes throughout His Word. They truly are "a lamp to my feet and a light to my path."[77] Let's use every Scriptural help God gives us to continue bravely our journey here below until we see the glories of Heaven with our own eyes.

---

76  2 Thessalonians 2:16-17
77  Psalms 119:105

# Be a Hero of the Faith!

Hebrews 11 is known as the "Great Heroes of the Faith" chapter in the Bible. After stating in the first verse that "faith is the assurance of things hoped for, the conviction of things not seen," the author of Hebrews then lists the servants of God that fit this criteria for faith: Abel, Abraham, Moses, and many others that cannot be mentioned "for time would fail me." Here is the common thread that unites all these saints together:

> These all died in faith, not having received the things promised, but having seen them and greeted them from afar, and having acknowledged that they were strangers and exiles on the earth. For people who speak thus make it clear that they are seeking a homeland. If they had been thinking of that land from which they had gone out, they would have had opportunity to return. But as it is, they desire a better country, that is, a heavenly one. Therefore God is not ashamed to be called their God, for he has prepared for them a city.[78]

Those of us who struggle with grief know that we

---

78 Hebrews 12:1

will not receive the "things promised" on this side of Heaven. The message of Hebrews is for all of us to encourage one another to strive to enter into the eternal rest that we have been promised. When we become overcome by sorrow, we are tempted to believe that this earth, this awful reality that we are living, is *all* that there is. What we forget is that we are strangers and exiles here, and we have to make it clear to others, but more importantly to ourselves, that we are journeying toward our homeland. We really don't have the option to travel "back to the land from which we have gone out." There is no returning to our previous lives in order to reclaim our loved ones from the grave. Instead, we need to seek a "better country, that is, a Heavenly one."

The promises of Heaven are real and true, and we need continual reminders of these promises in order to move forward toward this Celestial City where we will once again be reunited with our loved ones. How wonderful is it that despite all our doubts and unbelief, God will not be "ashamed to be called our God?" Let us greet that great Land "from afar" and look forward to the life to come.

# Running the Race

Immediately following the "Heroes of the Faith" chapter in the Book of Hebrews comes an astounding passage:

> Therefore, since we are surrounded
> by so great a cloud of witnesses, let
> us also lay aside every weight, and
> sin which clings so closely, and let us
> run with endurance the race that is
> set before us, looking to Jesus, the
> founder and perfecter of our faith,
> who for the joy that was set before
> him endured the cross, despising the
> shame, and is seated at the right hand
> of the throne of God.[79]

I was once taught that anytime you see the word "therefore" in the Bible, you should look to see what the "therefore" is there for. In most cases the preceding verse is the clue that unlocks the mystery:

> And all these, though commended
> through their faith, did not receive
> what was promised, since God had
> provided something better for us,

---

79 Hebrews 12:1

that apart from us they should not be made perfect.[80]

So the "heroes of the faith" are the "great cloud of witnesses" watching us from above. It's as though we are in a gigantic sports arena, "running with endurance the race that is set before us," and they are cheering us from the stands in Heaven. How encouraging is that image? Remember, these witnesses once ran the same race that we are now running—and they had their own cloud of cheerleaders rooting for them. Amazingly, one day we will be up in the stands as well, encouraging the generations of believers who come after us. What a privilege to be in that number!

As always, Jesus is the one we must keep our eyes on. He is the "founder and perfecter of our faith, who for the joy that was set before him endured the cross." We who are grieving the loss of a loved one have the best coach—one who is the man of sorrows and acquainted with grief. He suffered so much more than we ever will. Therefore, let us follow His great example and run our race, even though we may feel as if we have been sidelined by sadness. The joy of Heaven is set before us—what a glorious finish line!

---

80 Hebrews 11:39

# Who Sits Next to You in Church?

Let's take a look at one final passage in the Book of Hebrews:

> But you have come to Mount Zion and to the city of the living God, the heavenly Jerusalem, and to innumerable angels in festal gathering, and to the assembly of the firstborn who are enrolled in heaven, and to God, the judge of all, and to the spirits of the righteous made perfect, and to Jesus, the mediator of a new covenant, and to the sprinkled blood that speaks a better word than the blood of Abel.[81]

There is something about this passage that makes me excited and glad and grateful and amazed, all at once. It seems as though this is written to present day believers—even though it says that we have come to the heavenly Jerusalem now. How can that be? It must have something to do with worship— that somehow when we enter into that activity here on earth, we are also simultaneously entering into worship in Heaven. If that is the case, then our fellow worshipers are those that have gone ahead of us, namely our loved ones. Could it be that when we

---

81 Hebrews 12:22-24

sing and pray and read God's Word, that the person sitting next to us in the pew is the very one that has departed from us, the one whom we are missing so much?

My theory here seems to be supported by the ESV Study Bible, which states:

> This [passage] draws on extensive OT imagery of a new heavenly Zion/Jerusalem to say that Christian believers have access, in the invisible, spiritual realm, into the Heavenly Jerusalem, and therefore participate in worship with innumerable angels and the great assembly of those who have died in faith and are already in God's presence.[82]

Certainly the language of these verses confirms the reality of existence for those who have gone before us. The "assembly of the firstborn," for example, while initially referring to Christ, has been expanded to include all the heirs of salvation. Those "enrolled in Heaven" probably refers to the Book of Life referenced in several places in the Bible. And finally, "the spirits of the righteous made perfect" clearly refers to believers who were made righteous on earth because of Christ's work on the cross, but

---

82 ESV Study Bible, p. 2384

were made gloriously perfect upon their entrance into Heaven.

Of course, we should not be overly fixated on the fact that our family and friends in Heaven are worshiping together with us on Sunday mornings. The most important person we should be focusing on is Christ, "the mediator of a new covenant," who made all this possible. Without His sacrificial life and death, we wouldn't be excited and glad and grateful and amazed at all.

Thanks be to God for the incredible privilege of entering into Heavenly worship while we are still living as sojourners here on earth. Better still, one day we will experience the fullness of worship that we now know by faith alone; in just a little while, our faith will be sight!

# More Precious Than Gold

It's been said that "everything is perspective," and this is also true of grief. What we felt like and believed on Day One of our bereavement is different from Year One or Year Five. The further we are removed in time from the loss of our loved one, the bigger our perspective is of the entire experience. For most of us, our healing comes slowly, and our sense of joy more slowly still. But one day we will be able to see the "big picture" for what it is. There is a passage in 1 Peter 1 which helps us to keep the right perspective in the midst of our mourning:

> Blessed be the God and Father of our Lord Jesus Christ! According to his great mercy, he has caused us to be born again to a living hope through the resurrection of Jesus Christ from the dead, to an inheritance that is imperishable, undefiled, and unfading, kept in heaven for you, who by God's power are being guarded through faith for a salvation ready to be revealed in the last time. In this you rejoice, though now for a little while, if necessary, you have been grieved by various trials, so that the tested genuineness of your faith —more precious than gold that

perishes though it is tested by fire—
may be found to result in praise and
glory and honor at the revelation of
Jesus Christ.[83]

We know that we have been "grieved by various trials"; in fact, that has been the topic of this entire book. We have been tested beyond our limits, it seems, but it is our desire that this present affliction would result in "praise and glory and honor at the revelation of Jesus Christ." But is there really a reward for remaining faithful to God through this difficult time? Is there a light at the end of the tunnel?

Of course there is! These verses affirm that we have a living hope and an inheritance that cannot be taken away. Our hope is based on Christ's resurrection, which assures us of our own future resurrection and the resurrection of our loved ones. In fact, this hope is already stored in Heaven itself! What a beautiful picture of a future reality. We may despair and doubt and struggle with unbelief when we are in the midst of grief, but the eternal salvation of God's people has already been secured.

"Blessed be the God and Father of our Lord Jesus Christ!"

---

83  1 Peter 1:3-7

# Have Mercy

Throughout this entire book we have been assuming that one day we will see our loved ones in Heaven. But what if you aren't convinced that your daughter or mother or sister really accepted the gospel as presented in the Bible? What if you are unsure as to the eternal salvation of the one you are mourning? We've all been taught that as Christians we should not take or give false hope to those who are left behind with just ambiguous or confusing evidence of the faith of a departed loved one. What are we to do?

There is a very small verse in the book of Jude which might help. Very simply, it states:

And have mercy on those who doubt.[84]

Short of having a reliable "born-again-o-meter," we might not have perfect assurance that our loved one is in Heaven. This verse, though, gives hope to those who wonder. God is commanding us to have mercy on those who have doubts about matters of the faith. This verse certainly implies that God Himself is compassionate toward those who are plagued with skepticism or weakness or confusion. Why wouldn't we follow His good example?

---

84 Jude 1:22

After all, wasn't God merciful to us as we were coming to faith? God was certainly patient toward us when we were on our path toward belief. How do we know how far along our loved one might have been?

"The Lord is not slow to fulfill his promise as some count slowness, but is patient toward you, not wishing that any should perish, but that all should reach repentance."[85]

Let us be merciful as God is merciful.

---

85  2 Peter 3:9

# Endurance

It has been said that Revelation, the final book of the Bible, is one of the most difficult books of Scripture to understand. That is a well-deserved reputation, which should make us cautious in interpreting it. Nonetheless, Revelation contains some of the clearest passages on Heavenly realities found in the Bible. For instance:

> Here is a call for the endurance of the saints, those who keep the commandments of God and their faith in Jesus. And I heard a voice from heaven saying, "Write this: Blessed are the dead who die in the Lord from now on." "Blessed indeed," says the Spirit, "that they may rest from their labors, for their deeds follow them!"[86]

Anyone who has experienced the loss of a loved one knows about endurance. Every daily action calls for deliberate endurance: getting out of bed in the morning, showing up at work, answering phone calls, making dinner. The most routine tasks seem insurmountable when we are weighed down with grief.

---

86 Revelation 14:12-13

But endurance in the faith is even more of a battle. We are so disappointed in God's providence, so anxious about others, so fearful that someone else will be taken from us. Our minds are too confused to study the Bible and too distracted to focus on Sunday morning worship. Our hearts break with sorrow and our bodies hurt with various pains. And prayer? When we try, we can barely eke out a "Help me, God!"

How can we endure? By focusing our attention on the second of these verses. God is telling us to persevere because we have great treasures stored up in Heaven. Those of us who keep the commandments of God and our faith, weak though it may be, will eventually have rest from all our labors. God is telling us here that we are blessed; in fact, He says that twice in this passage. We should believe that we *are* blessed, and that we *will be* blessed, if we endure until the end.

What we do here on earth is mysteriously carried over into the next life. We only have glimpses as to how this will be manifested—but everything in the Bible is true. Our deeds will follow us. There is some level of continuity between our lives here on earth and our lives in Heaven. Our loved ones understand this now, while we can only imagine. So we read and believe what God has promised, and so we let our souls be encouraged. A voice from

Heaven has spoken to us, and we look forward to the rest from our labors that awaits us.

*Praise God from Whom All Blessings Flow.*

# The Grand Finale

We have come to the last stop on this journey through the Scriptures. My goal in writing this book was to comfort you in your grief with the reality of Heaven. With Revelation 21 we have arrived at the most famous of all afterlife passages. I'm guessing that probably half of the sympathy cards I received after my son's death quoted at least some of the following verses:

> Then I saw a new heaven and a new earth, for the first heaven and the first earth had passed away, and the sea was no more. And I saw the holy city, new Jerusalem, coming down out of heaven from God, prepared as a bride adorned for her husband. And I heard a loud voice from the throne saying, "Behold, the dwelling place of God is with man. He will dwell with them, and they will be his people, and God himself will be with them as their God. He will wipe away every tear from their eyes, and death shall be no more, neither shall there be mourning, nor crying, nor pain anymore, for the former things have passed away."[87]

---

87 Revelation 21:1-4

Having grown up in Massachusetts and then residing in Southern New Hampshire for many years, I became accustomed to the phrase: "Reverse the Curse." Any baseball fan would recognize this as the attempt of the Red Sox to overcome an eighty-seven-year drought of winning the World Series. That finally happened in 2004.

When I become a Christian in early adulthood, the phrase "Reverse the Curse" took on an entirely different meaning for me, which is epitomized by this portion of Scripture. On the cross, through Christ's death and resurrection, the curse of our sin is eliminated. His work repaired the breach between man and God, allowing us access into Heavenly realms. The ultimate thrill will be when death is no more; when death is dead, there will be "no more mourning, nor crying, nor pain anymore." The curse will be completely reversed. Isn't that what we long for now?

Long ago Adam and Eve were privileged to walk with God in the Garden of Eden, and one day we will be granted that same delight. Our loved ones are experiencing this wonderful reality right now; they are in complete fellowship with the Lord of Lords and King of Kings. "And God Himself will be with them as their God."

God has already wiped every tear from our loved

one's eyes; shouldn't that image help wipe away ours as well?